LICK 'EM, STICK 'EM

LICK 'EM, STICK 'EM
THE LOST ART OF POSTER STAMPS
H. THOMAS STEELE

ABBEVILLE PRESS · PUBLISHERS · NEW YORK

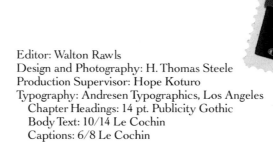

DEDICATED

to the passionate collector — may
your passion become your work
and may your work become
your passion.

Editor: Walton Rawls
Design and Photography: H. Thomas Steele
Production Supervisor: Hope Koturo
Typography: Andresen Typographics, Los Angeles
   Chapter Headings: 14 pt. Publicity Gothic
   Body Text: 10/14 Le Cochin
   Captions: 6/8 Le Cochin

PAGE 1

AN ATTRACTIVE FEMALE MOTORIST ENTICES
PROSPECTIVE CUSTOMERS TO A 1915
AUTO SHOW.

PAGE 2

AN ILLINOIS PRINTER SELLS LITHOGRAPHY
VIA AN EARLY POSTER STAMP, THE
MINI-BILLBOARD.

Library of Congress Cataloging-in-Publication Data
Steele, H. Thomas, 1953-
   Lick 'em, stick 'em: the lost art of poster stamps/
   H. Thomas Steele.
    p.   cm.
   ISBN 0-89659-899-3 : $19.95
   1.   Poster stamps.   I.   Title.
NC1855.S84   1989   88-38951
741.67--dc19   CIP

TABLE OF CONTENTS

AS I FORAGED ONCE AGAIN in the lush fields of the visual and graphic arts, I was astounded to come upon yet another area of printed ephemera that has remained uncataloged until now. My newest find was a form of lithography that sprang up around the turn of the century and produced some of the most beautiful and accessible communications artwork I have ever seen. An impetuous scavenger of graphics, I was somewhat taken aback that this naive form of advertising had eluded my awareness until recently.

A few years ago, I was enticed into attending a stamp show, all the while thinking, "Show me something I haven't seen before." Stamp collectors, it seemed to me, were interested in just the official POSTAGE stamps issued as a source of revenue for the distribution of the mail.

Stamps that are not denominated for revenue are known as "Cinderellas" or non-postage stamps, and the most common examples today are Christmas and Easter seals. Telegraph stamps, locals, charity seals, and exhibition labels are

THE ART OF POSTER STAMP DESIGN IS CELEBRATED IN A VIVID PALETTE OF PAINTS AND BRUSHES.

other Cinderellas. But just as Cinderella was prevented from going to the ball, so Cinderella stamps have been excluded from most philatelic catalogs, exhibitions, and displays. Nevertheless, the wares of one lonely dealer in Cinderellas caught my fancy. He was showing advertising seals, or poster stamps, and their freshness of design and brilliance of color were unlike anything I'd seen before, except in the work of the early poster artists from Germany and Austria. As it turns out, the heyday of poster stamps was the decades from 1890 to 1940, the same era that spawned the European poster artists. Many of these stamps, generally gummed and perforated, were dated to prove that fact. For me, a small sampling has grown into a large collection.

Having the showcase of a book to share the wealth of this particular offshoot of graphic arts is satisfying to this collector's soul. If you enjoy the thrill of the hunt, the field of poster stamps still has many neglected princesses awaiting rescue from the cinders.

—H. Thomas Steele

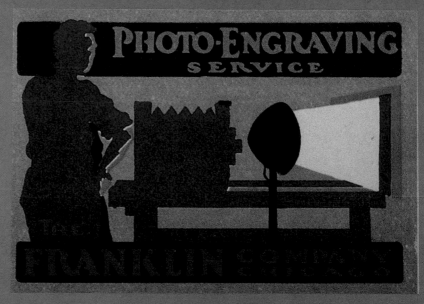

THE FRANKLIN COMPANY OF CHICAGO TOUTED ITS FULL RANGE OF CUSTOMER SERVICES IN THIS SERIES OF
STAMPS PRINTED ON ONE SHEET. NOTE THE ADVENTUROUS USE OF COLOR COMBINATIONS, CIRCA 1915.

A NEW FORMAT IN GRAPHICS and advertising caught the eye of the world at the turn of the century. Miniscule in size, universal in appeal, and blazing with all the varied colors of the rainbow, this was the poster stamp, an esoteric rarity among collectibles. As the name suggests, it is a poster in stamp form. Always gummed and a little larger than the regular postage variety, these stamps normally were printed up in perforated sheets so they could easily be torn apart and stuck to invoices, envelopes, and correspondence, or simply collected as sheets into albums. In the name of art, commerce, and even propaganda, the poster stamp presented diminutively all that the largest billboard displayed, accomplishing everything that is required of an efficient poster. Although not issued for revenue, this "currency of commerce" presented immense opportunities both for the vision of the graphic artist and the keen businessman.

Germany created poster stamps or "REKLAME

AUSTRIAN POSTER ARTIST BERTHOLD LÖFFLER DISPLAYS HIS UNIQUE STYLE, 1908.

MARKEN" (literally "advertising stamps") around 1907, just as that country had previously pioneered the fancy post card. Munich, Nuremberg, and Cologne all claimed the honor of having originated this new medium. Its sole reason for existence was to advertise and promote a product or event.

Up until this time, the only stamps produced were revenue or postage, and those usually were intricate, single-color etchings or line engravings. Exhibition seals issued in the late 1800s were considered the forerunners of the colorful poster stamp, as were the earlier chromolithographic trade cards. The new poster stamp, with its vivid splash of brilliant colors, was a bold contrast to the drab black-and-white graphic landscape that was permissible at the time among most distinguished lines of business.

The attraction of poster stamps is the eye-catching poster art itself. Although derivative of posters, many of these stamps were designed specifically for use at this small size, never to be seen any larger. The French lithographer and artist

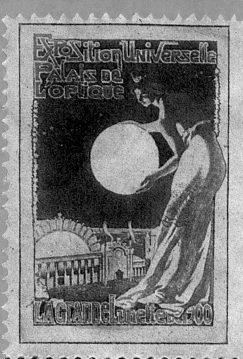

THE PARIS WORLD EXPOSITION EMPLOYED THE TALENT OF LOCAL ARTISTS TO ADVERTISE THE UPCOMING 1900 EVENT IN THE PREVAILING ART NOUVEAU STYLE. PRINTING TECHNOLOGY OF THE TIME LIMITED THIS STAMP TO MONOCHROME.

Jules Chéret, who is considered the father of the modern poster, was among the first to adapt art to advertising in a big way, creating stellar graphics for such clients as the Moulin Rouge and the Pálais de Glace. Along with fellow artists Alphonse Mucha, Toulouse-Lautrec, and others, Chéret lavished a new palette of riotous color on the streets and boulevards of Paris, creating posters replete with dancing figures and explosive, kinetic imagery. Germany, too, had its share of talented poster artists, though of a different vision. Ludwig Hohlwein, Lucian Bernhard, and the Austrian-born Julius Klinger were among the foremost poster artists of the day, and many of their graphics were reduced to poster stamp size for use on envelopes, cards, or invoices to attract attention to some upcoming event or to promote some product. The influence of these artists was enormous, but it was the mostly anonymous commercial illustrators of that time whose unsung work is featured in this book.

The first poster stamps in Germany were issued around 1907 by a large food-product manufacturer to popularize his brands. Every letter, package, and price list carried one of the company's stamps. The brilliant colorings and clever designs caught the consumers' eye, and soon this firm was overwhelmed by requests for the stamps themselves. This demand was

ADOLFO HOHENSTEIN, THE PREMIER POSTER ARTIST IN ITALY AT THE TURN OF THE CENTURY, DESIGNED THIS POSTER STAMP WITH STATUESQUE GODDESSES FOR AN 1899 ELECTRICAL EXPOSITION, COMMEMORATING THE BIRTH OF PHYSICIST ALESSANDRO VOLTA.

promptly met by their publishing a set of eight stamps, each one exploiting a separate brand of goods. In order to reach more of the public, the manufacturer included a coupon in each package sent out, informing the purchaser of how to receive his own full set of stamps. A German chocolate manufacturer reproduced several of his most popular posters in miniature stamp form, gummed and perforated. In each penny packet of chocolate, he inserted one of these stamps. Children were soon buying the chocolate just to get the stamp, much as collectors today buy bubble gum for the baseball cards. Other businesses followed this lead, and in less than six months poster stamps were in general use throughout Germany. A coffee roaster began to distribute stamps. Electric light companies found these stamps to be an effective method of calling attention to the advantages of electricity. A biscuit company produced a series of twelve stamps, each one displaying the various operations in the manufacture of its product. Virtually everyone, the butcher, the baker, and the candlestick maker, had stamps printed to advertise themselves and their handiwork. Great steamship lines and railroad companies as well as other venerable and dignified concerns joined the publicity push. By 1914 over five thousand different designs of poster stamps were being issued in Germany alone, as print-

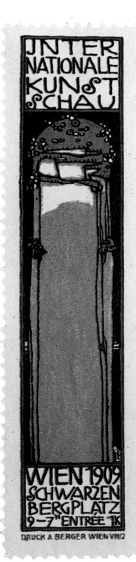

HISTORICALLY VALUABLE POSTER STAMPS SHOW MARKEDLY DISTINCT STYLES OF GRAPHICS FROM THE VIENNESE SECESSIONISTS TO THE GEOMETRY OF EMIL PIRCHAN'S DIE BRÜCKE TO THE ORGANIC HAND-DRAWN QUALITY OF EARLY ART NOUVEAU.

HANS RUDI ERDT, A LEADING GERMAN POSTERIST, DESIGNED THIS
HANDSOME STAMP FOR AN INTERNATIONAL TRAVEL SHOW IN BERLIN.

ing presses groaned under the burden of this new advertising medium.

Early in this century, there was evidence of artistic progress and development everywhere. This was manifest in the truly remarkable productivity in Europe of both artists and printers from 1908 until the outbreak of war in 1914. Many artists with an international clientele shared common design formulas and styles, but World War I closed the design borders, and poster styles became markedly nationalistic in character. Immediately following the war, poster artists, curious to see what their foreign competitors were producing, derived renewed exuberance and vitality for their craft from influences all around Europe. From Germany the success of advertising stamps spread rapidly into Austria, Italy, Holland, France, and England. In each of these nations poster stamps received the same enthusiastic reception. The French printer Delandre, in the four eventful years from 1914 through 1917, produced one of the most dramatic and artistic arrays of military vignettes and propaganda seals the world had seen, enlisting some of the finest artists and military experts to create such stamps.

American printers and advertisers were well aware of the high quality and productivity of European presses, but apparently they viewed the poster as just an offshoot of the efficient realism of their

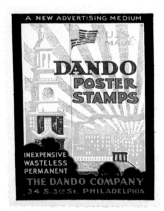 

TWO EARLY POSTER STAMPS FROM PRINTERS WHO WERE
INSTRUMENTAL IN SPREADING THE WORD AND THE MEDIUM.

A SERIES OF GERMAN STAMPS (TWO OF TEN SHOWN) DEPICTING
THE HISTORY OF TRANSPORTATION, WITH THE ONE ON FUTURE
SPACE TRAVEL (THEN MERELY A CONCEPT) FAIRLY ACCURATE.

ALPHONSE MUCHA DESIGNED THIS POSTER FOR THE
REGIONAL FAIR AT HIS BIRTHPLACE, IVANCICE,
SHOWING WOMEN IN REGIONAL COSTUME.

monochromatic magazine advertisements. America's need for and use of posters—except during World War I—was never on as high a scale of deployment as throughout Europe. But poster stamps preceded even the matchbook cover in terms of advertising effectiveness.

Attention to poster stamps in the United States was first attracted by a series of graphic stamps produced by the Munro & Harford Printing Company for the North German Lloyd Steamship Company in early 1914. The German influence had crossed the Atlantic, and large printers and lithographers knew a good thing when they saw it. Aggressive commercial artists along with engravers and manufacturers of gummed paper solicited work via self-promotional poster stamps. Publishers Printing, Robert Gair Company, Dando, and Wentz & Co. produced stamps and pamphlets announcing that they had

gone into the business of manufacturing advertising stamps. This new industry was beginning to grow to very large proportions. In response to printers' publicity releases, large quantities of orders were received from such top concerns as Lehigh Valley Railroad, Postal Life Insurance, Funk & Wagnalls, and Ballantine & Sons. Rogers & Company printed an excellent series of stamps for the American Book Company.

The year 1915 seems to have been a high-water mark for the hobby. Poster stamps were displayed at a merchandise show in Madison Square Garden, and

TYPOGRAPHY AND DESIGN WERE KEY INGREDIENTS
IN TWO APPROACHES SHOWN ABOVE, BUT NOTE THE
STYLISTIC CHANGE IN ONLY EIGHT YEARS' TIME.

THE POSTER STAMP BULLETIN was published in Yonkers, New York, for a growing number of enthusiasts in that area. The Society of Modern Art, catering mainly to the graphic arts, printed THE POSTER ART STAMP SUPPLEMENT, which contained many examples of art posters in stamp form. The market was flooded with millions of flakes of brightly hued paper as clubs and societies formed to collect and preserve the humble poster stamp.

The poster stamp made possible the novel use of brilliant color in advertising to attract the stoic eye. Every known process was employed in producing them—lithography, three- and four-color process, zinc and copper-plate etching, steel engraving, and photogravure. While European varieties from the Belle Epoque and the Secessionist eras were even embossed, lithography and the printing of broad, flat areas of color were responsible for the most striking graphic examples.

Increasing business through advertising simplicity was the main intent of poster stamps, but they also brought high art to the masses on a level that could never have been achieved otherwise. Poster stamps were the common man's art gallery. Adults as well as children were charmed by the stamps from the very beginning, collecting and pasting them into books specially made for that purpose. It was possible for the layman, with a minimum amount of effort and practically no expense, to accumulate a much finer collection of posters than he could buy in any larger format. They were widely considered handsome works of decorative art even then and truly worthy of being sought after for permanent possession. Inherent in the poster stamp's format was the suggestion of value—beyond its worth as art—for postage stamps have a secondary value even after cancellation that mainstream stamp collectors are quite familiar with. And after a long hiatus, poster stamps are being collected again, though as part of a group called "Cinderellas," the neglected stepsisters of true stamp collecting. But you remember what eventually happened to Cinderella!

Poster stamps spoke a universal tongue—the language of communication. They expressed a symbol, furthered propaganda, created historical sug-

INSPIRING CONCEPT AND EXECUTION, COMBINED WITH RICH, EYE-CATCHING COLOR, MAKE
THIS SERIES OF COLLECTIBLE PRINTER'S STAMPS VERY EFFECTIVE ADVERTISING.

gestions, ensured duties, drove home responsibilities, advertised utilities, suggested service, impressed a slogan, or merely shared comfort and cheer—all at a glance. Through the wizardry of the artist, the spell of the writer, and the mesmerizing use of eye-catching color, the result was just plain great advertising.

Effectiveness of communication relied upon the principles of good graphic design to carry the image or message to the viewer. Although design can be highly subjective, the universal appeal of poster stamps recognized design as an integral element of this new advertising medium. The public took notice of the new use of imaginative color combinations that were in bold contrast to the monochromatic magazine ads prevalent during the first two decades of this century. Germany gave us the capabilities of full-color reproduction with the advent of new presses and printing technologies, but their famous poster artists also contributed greatly to our visual design education, leaving us lessons of integrated simplicity. European graphic artists simplified the swirling curves and ornamentation of the preceding Art Nouveau and Beaux Arts periods and created a whole new vocabulary for the visual arts. It was the simplicity of shape, form, and color that caught everyone's attention. Advertisers had only a few seconds to grab someone's attention, and the best way to compete with the daily barrage of visuals was to simplify the elements and shock the viewers with color, leaving them wanting to know more but remembering what was seen. A sense of humor was often employed to create memorable images, for a good concept that made people think about a product in a different way would tend to reinforce the design. Whether designers used a long-necked giraffe to sell neckties or a sleepy child hugging a tire ("time to retire—Fisk Tires"), the images were positively retained in the mind's eye, which is the goal of classic advertising. Advertising as an image-making process had begun. Intelligent businessmen sought the aid of the poster stamp to give the public something interesting and attractive to look at—and at the same time identify their companies' name with. Business value was the first consideration, but taste levels had developed and improved so much from

1910 to 1920 that business firms were competing not only in advertising but also in educational and aesthetic matters, and the demand for an artistic approach was on the rise.

As national subscription magazines entered homes throughout America and elsewhere in the 1920s and '30s, businesses sought a larger piece of the advertising pie. Effective advertising meant reaching the largest possible market. Although poster stamps had made incredible inroads, it began to be felt that advertising dollars were better spent on full-page, full-color ads in high-circulation publications that offered plenty of room for informative copy rather than on the minimalist, small-scale poster stamps. Even though there were exposition stamps and seals for the various world's fairs and events of the 1930s, as well as propaganda stamps issued in the early 1940s to boost patriotism at the beginning of World War II, the days of poster stamps were clearly numbered.

Classic design comes from the heart and soul. A beautiful poster stamp can be broken down into various elements that may suggest why a particular example works on the level of design, such as its innovative use of negative space, daring sense of color, imaginative typography, or harmoniously balanced layout; but the total piece is greater than the sum of

its parts. Early poster stamp artists drew upon an innate talent to transpose what they saw onto a miniature canvas in a new way, not necessarily relying on what had come before. The stamps revealed much of the man behind the design as well as the product it was advertising. These anonymous, unheralded designers have left us a legacy that ranks high with any other form of folk or commercial art yet produced by popular culture.

In an era when letter writing was still treasured, the most intimate form of personal expression became a vehicle of the advertising industry for publicity. Poster stamps rode on envelopes like contraband—a master stroke of advertising genius in a pre-media age, as thousands of companies and organizations routinely affixed them to their correspondence and brochures as an added medium of communication. Whether reduced from a large poster or designed specifically to be used in miniature, literally millions of poster stamps were magnificently printed by craftsmen of what is now a bygone era. Many examples have been lost to time, but for now you should feast your eyes on these visual remnants of popular, turn-of-the-century Americana—where the middle class met the art world, when less really was more, where collectible poster stamps were the "confetti of commerce."

THERE WAS NO BETTER WAY TO ADVERTISE YOUR SERVICES THAN TO PRODUCE A POSTER STAMP FOR YOUR OWN TARGET AUDIENCE. THESE STAMPS MAY HAVE BEEN THE FIRST FULL-COLOR BUSINESS CARDS THAT NOT ONLY SAID WHO YOU WERE BUT SHOWED WHAT YOU DID.

WHILE THEY FLOURISHED, poster stamps were traded and valued much like postage stamps. Hundreds of collector clubs were formed here in the United States and abroad. Although production of these stamps and interest in them fell off markedly over the last half century, a stirring of renewed excitement appears to be in the making. The Poster Stamp Society of America was formed in 1987 to the delight of a small but sincere group of collectors. At recent stamp shows around the country, poster stamps are resurfacing with steadily increasing prices. The highest values for these rediscovered gems go to signed copies by well-known European and American artists in both the fine art and commercial fields: Ludwig Hohlwein, Julius Klinger, Lucian Bernhard, and Alphonse Mucha to name a few. The illustrators Edward Penfield, J.C. Leyendecker, Maxfield Parrish, and others were leading the American pack while in England Frank Newbould, E. McKnight Kauffer, and Tom Purvis came to the

THE VENERABLE STUDIO OF LUCIAN BERNHARD AND HANS ROSEN WAS HIRED TO CREATE THIS COMPELLING IMAGE FOR THE BERLIN ADVERTISING EXHIBITION OF 1929.

fore due to the early influence of the Beggarstaffs. It was the fine artists of the time who best understood the requirements of good poster design and the essentials of working with flat colors. The painters and draftsmen of this genre recognized that an essential prerequisite for a successful promotion was to restrict elements to the bare fundamentals. New standards were developed in the use of color that still are accepted today, but they were considered bold and brazen for the time. Advertisers at the turn of the century were as much concerned with space limitations and distribution costs as they are today, but poster stamps could be produced in large quantities at a low cost, and their distribution would be practically free. Popular culture accepted these artists and their stamps with open arms and empty stamps albums to fill. America caught on with the importation of modern German printing presses around 1910. Madison Avenue advertising men eager to find new ways to sell products sped the poster stamp revolution along.

Ludwig Hohlwein's masterful poster stamp for Munich's summerfest embodies all that a classic poster should be. Singular conceptual design, bold painting, and legible, well-placed typography combine to turn the head and move the soul.

ARROW *White* SHIRTS

with laundered cuffs. The shirt of the well dressed business man

$1.50 and $2.00

CLUETT, PEABODY & CO. Inc. Makers

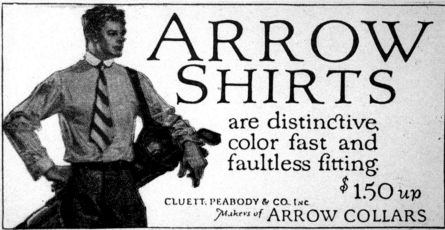

ARROW SHIRTS

are distinctive, color fast and faultless fitting.

$1.50 up

CLUETT, PEABODY & CO. Inc.
Makers of ARROW COLLARS

ARROW *Business* SHIRTS

The label is the indicator to dependable style and quality

Red Label   Black Label   Blue Label
$1.50 $2.00 $2.50 up

CLUETT, PEABODY & CO., INC., Troy, N.Y.
Makers of ARROW COLLARS

"GET THE HABIT"

GO TO

Brill Brothers

ABOVE: THIS STAMP FROM THE BRILL BROTHERS RETAIL CLOTHIERS DISPLAYS THEIR FAMOUS SLOGAN. THE STAMP'S DESIGNER WAS MAXFIELD PARRISH, WHO WOULD ALSO BECOME FAMOUS ON HIS OWN.

LEFT: J.C. LEYENDECKER'S CHIC ARROW SHIRT MAN WAS THE EPITOME OF STYLE AND GOOD TASTE IN THE TWENTIES, AT WORK, AT PLAY, AND AT REST.

LEFT: AUDI AUTOMOBILES ARE
POSTERIZED BY LUDWIG HOHLWEIN,
WITH CONTEMPORARY USE OF A
DESIGN GRID, 1912. RIGHT: FRANZ PAUL
GLASS CONSTRUCTS AN IMMEDIATE
SYMBOL—AT HAND AN EXHIBITION OF
BAVARIAN HANDICRAFTS.

RIGHT: MAN DREAMS OF FLYING IN
THIS SIMPLE AND HEROIC
COMPOSITION. LUDWIG HOHLWEIN
MAKES THE DREAM REALITY.

ABOVE LEFT: DYNAMIC COMPOSITION AND EXOTIC SIGHTS CREATE EFFECTIVE COMMUNICATION IN LUDWIG HOHLWEIN'S TRAVEL POSTER FOR LLOYD-BREMEN MEDITERRANEAN CRUISES, 1913. ABOVE: SHINING WHITE TEA CUPS ARE THE FOCAL POINT OF THIS POSTER STAMP. STRONG DESIGN AND ARRESTING COLOR ARE THE HALLMARKS OF HOHLWEIN'S GRAPHICS, 1910.

LEFT: YOU CAN ALMOST TASTE THE EXOTICALLY PREPARED PHEASANT DISH IN THIS STAMP BY BERTHOLD LÖFFLER FOR A CULINARY EXHIBITION, 1914.

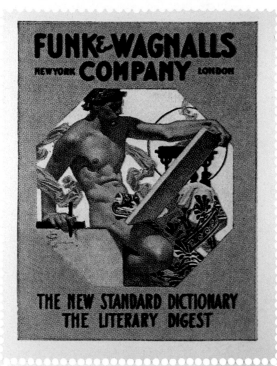

FUNK & WAGNALLS CHOSE TOP ILLUSTRATORS TO ADVERTISE THEIR NEW DICTIONARY IN 1913. ABOVE LEFT: ALPHONSE MUCHA.
ABOVE RIGHT: J.C. LEYENDECKER. BELOW LEFT: EDWARD PENFIELD. BELOW RIGHT: MAXFIELD PARRISH.

ABOVE: FRANK NEWBOULD, THE
RENOWNED ENGLISH POSTER ARTIST, GIVES
US TWO WHIMSICAL APPROACHES FOR
HOME EXHIBITIONS. LEFT: LUCIAN
BERNHARD SHOWS US JUST HOW THREE-
DIMENSIONAL A TWO-DIMENSIONAL SPOOL
OF KNITTING YARN CAN LOOK.

ABOVE: ROCKWELL KENT LENDS AN ARTISTIC HAND AND A POLITICAL VOICE TO THIS POWERFUL DRAWING. LEFT: HART SCHAFFNER & MARX HAD THE GOOD TASTE TO ENLIST EDWARD PENFIELD TO PAINT A SERIES OF TEN SCENES INVOLVING COSTUME THROUGH THE AGES.

ABOVE: THE STATUE OF AN IRONWORKER PRESIDES OVER THE CITY OF LIEGE, CELEBRATING 100 YEARS OF BELGIAN INDEPENDENCE, BY HUB DUP. LEFT: RARE POSTER STAMP BY EGON SCHIELE FROM A 1912 MUSIC FESTIVAL DISPLAYS HIS UNIQUE DRAFTSMANSHIP.

GERMANY GETS THE CREDIT for creating the concept of a small advertising poster stamp. While Paris was already enchanted by the ebullient posters of Lautrec and Chéret, Germany was an artistic latecomer. The beginning of the change in German poster art was spread by the vanguard of new ideas prevalent in the avant-garde publications founded around the turn of the century. In particular, the Secessionists espoused the obliteration of the barriers between life and art, that art should have a social purpose and influence people, and that there should be no limits on the development of art. As a result, posters reflected the trends in art at the time: Art Nouveau, Bauhaus, Realism, Suprematism, Constructivism, and various other "isms." Individual artists were largely responsible for local exhibitions and advertising for political parties and other interest groups. Although it prompted another point of view, political agitation resulted in the progressive development of advertising forms. The mostly typographic poster owes an artistic debt to great German typographers such as Lucian Bernhard, Fritz Ehmcke, and Willy Petzold. Images and words were reduced to utter simplicity and maximum impact. The effect of this bold approach was felt in neighboring countries throughout Europe. Italy, France, England, and the smaller countries caught this design fever and produced challenging visuals of similar beauty for nationalistic products and businesses that were subtly altered to reflect artistic trends and styles within their own borders. The course of development in the art of poster stamps encompassed roughly forty years. In Germany it ended in 1939 as Nazi control was sharply intensified and free artistic expression was no longer possible. World War II marked the decline of poster stamps for the rest of Europe as well as for the United States.

FRANZ VON STUCK'S SURREALIST MOTIF CAUGHT EUROPE'S EYE, WITH CLASSICAL GREEK ARCHITECTURE TO FRAME THE TYPOGRAPHY, 1911.

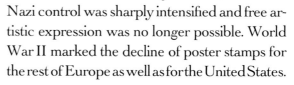

A CLASSIC EXAMPLE OF EARLY GERMAN POSTER ART IN DESIGN COMPOSITION, COLOR, AND COMPLETE COMMAND OF THE PRINTING PROCESS. BACKGROUND BECOMES FOREGROUND IN THIS WORK BY HANS RUDI ERDT, 1913.

ABOVE: A PRIME EXAMPLE OF THE
SOPHISTICATED MARRIAGE OF DESIGN
AND TYPOGRAPHY FOR THE EAST &
WEST INDIES EXHIBITION, 1928. LEFT:
THE HEROIC FIGURE AND
COMPLEMENTARY COLORS IN THIS
POSTER BY LEOPOLDO METLICOVITZ
SHOW HIS UNIQUE APPROACH TO
POSTER ART AND THE INFLUENCE OF
JUGENDSTIL, CIRCA 1900.

ABOVE: STYLIZED
FIGURES ARE USED IN
THREE COLOR
VARIATIONS FOR A
GERMAN HOME AND
GARDEN SHOW. NOTE
FRENCH ART DECO
INFLUENCE. RIGHT:
THE GRANDEUR OF
NATURALISTIC
CLASSICISM SHOWS
OFF THE VERSATILITY
OF LEOPOLDO
METLICOVITZ, 1907.
FAR RIGHT: THE
PINNACLE OF
FRENCH ART DECO,
FEATURING A FEMALE
EARTH GODDESS
BLESSING THE FRUITS
OF THE LAND.

ABOVE: THE WHITE GLOVE APPROACH BY HANS RUDI ERDT TO THE PROBLEMATIC JOB OF SELLING IRONICALLY NAMED CIGARETTES, CIRCA 1912. FAR LEFT: A TRIANGULAR GROUPING OF PRETZELS BY LUDWIG HOHLWEIN POINTS THE WAY TO A HEALTHY GERMAN SNACK, 1913. LEFT: THE BLACK-AND-WHITE STYLE OF GERMAN DESIGNER WILLY PETZOLD WEAVES THE WEB FOR A 1924 TEXTILE EXHIBITION.

ABOVE: TIMELESS DESIGN SPANNED THE BORDERS OF EUROPE, AS IN
THESE ATTENTION-GRABBERS FROM PROMINENT POSTER ARTISTS.

ABOVE: These stop signs demanded the attention of
European consumers and the interest of hobbyists.

FAR LEFT: FOUR WAGNERIAN OPERAS ARE ILLUSTRATED TOGETHER, UTILIZING THE ECONOMY OF A THREE-COLOR PRESS RUN. LEFT: THE SIMPLIFIED COLORATION OF A LEOPOLDO METLICOVITZ POSTER, 1907.

LEFT: GERMANIC MYTHOLOGICAL SYMBOLS ARE USED TO ANNOUNCE UPCOMING EXHIBITIONS.

ADVANCES IN EUROPEAN PRINTING technology reached American shores in the first decade of the 1900s. One offspring of this aspect of the Industrial Revolution was the miniature poster stamp, which lent the grace and charm of its various colors and designs to otherwise dreary and emotionless printed matter. The American advertising industry, although in its infancy, was the instigator and stimulus for poster stamps, and American businesses were the beneficiary. The poster stamp merged the economic and cultural elite. Business profited from a narrative art full of wit and technical achievement, while art on a deadline found itself heavily endowed financially. Companies copied the competition and looked for new sensory avenues to get their products and ideas across to the public. Poster stamps were the vehicle. Although distributed by the millions, poster stamp advertising was considered one of the least expensive and most successful methods of early advertising, as the space it occupied did not have to be purchased. In advance of even the earliest advertising matchcovers, they were an effective, cost-efficient means of reaching a wide audience with an aesthetic approach. Through stimulating imagery, advertisers enticed the public into coveting continually new and unfamiliar luxuries and pleasures as well as changing social viewpoints. There was nothing to compete or conflict with a poster stamp's message where it was affixed. Issued at regular intervals, the stamps ensured the gradual yet steady assimilation of their subject matter by both children and adults. Poster stamps were stuck onto all business correspondence; letters, envelopes, statements, or invoices bore colorful illustrations of special services or new products.

ADVERTISERS WERE QUICK TO EXPLOIT THE MYSTIQUE OF AMERICA'S EARLY DAYS, CHOOSING TO SHOW AN INDIAN CHIEF RATHER THAN THE SHOES THEY WERE INTENDING TO SELL.

Where other methods of approach—including the door-to-door salesman—had failed, these stamps got inside the front doors of American homes. Pictures told more than any pitchman could pitch.

MAKERS
SINCE
1870

FIRE
HOSE

BOSTON WOVEN HOSE & RUBBER C°

PRODUCT ENDORSEMENT HAS LONG BEEN A PLOY OF ADVERTISERS; HERE A BRAVE
FIREMAN ASCENDS THROUGH SMOKE AND FLAMES WITH HIS DEPENDABLE FIRE HOSE.

RIGHT: LITERAL
INTERPRETATION
OF THE PRODUCT
AND BRIGHT
COLOR
OVERSHADOW
THE QUESTION OF
WHY SWANS ARE
HOLDING PENS IN
THE FIRST PLACE.
FAR RIGHT:
POINTING OUT
THE NEED FOR A
PRODUCT WILL
ALSO SELL IT.

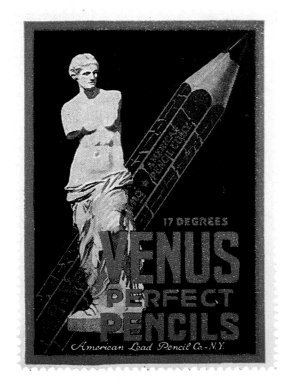

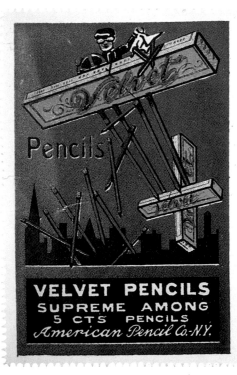

LEFT: A PLAYFUL
WAY OF
ILLUSTRATING
PENCILS IN AN ERA
WHEN MOST
SCHOOLCHILDREN
USED PENCIL
BOXES. FAR LEFT:
ALTHOUGH THE
ARMLESS VENUS
DE MILO COULD
NOT USE THEM,
THE ANALOGY OF
HER PERFECTION
WAS STILL
EMPLOYED TO
SELL THESE
PENCILS.

ABOVE: A MOVIE DIRECTOR'S APPROACH TO TAMPA ORANGE GROVES PICTURES THEM FROM LONG SHOT TO MEDIUM SHOT TO CLOSE UP.

THE CARPENTER, TO MAKE THINGS TIGHT TAKES SIMONDS SAWS, MECHANICALLY RIGHT

ABOVE: A STICKER WITH TEETH SELLS ATKINS BLADES THAT SAW THROUGH THE COMPETITION. RIGHT: NO BUSINESS COULD SELL A PRODUCT MECHANICALLY DEFECTIVE, BUT SIMONDS GUARANTEES THEIR SAWS TO BE ANYTHING BUT.

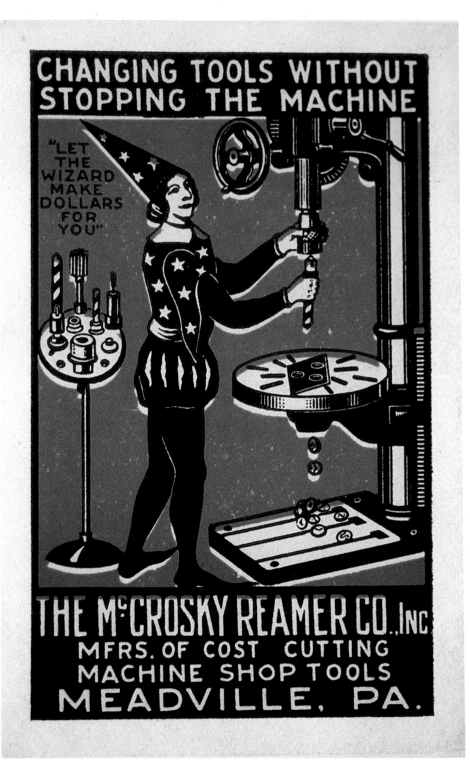

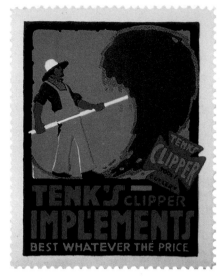

TOP: IT'S A HOEDOWN AT THE HAYSTACK, BUT HAY WAS NEVER THAT COLOR. ABOVE: WHO BUT U.S. CARTRIDGES WOULD TRUST A GOATEED MAN IN A CHECKERED BERET TO SELL AMMUNITION? LEFT: AS TECHNOLOGY ENGINEERED NEW MACHINES, THE MAGIC OF POSTER STAMPS EDUCATED INQUIRING MINDS.

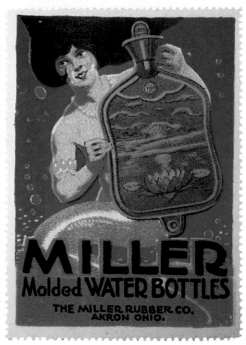

ABOVE, FROM THE LEFT: THE ONLY PRUDENT WAY TO SHOW THIS PRODUCT; FREUDIAN-LOOKING DOCTOR PERFORMS PSYCHIC SURGERY; MERMAID UNDER WATER DISPLAYS A WATER BOTTLE THAT DOES NOT LEAK–STRANGE IMAGERY FOR A RUBBER COMPANY. RIGHT: AFFORDABLE CAT'S PAW HEELS THAT LAND YOU ON YOUR FEET. FAR RIGHT: LAMPS FOR LATE-NIGHT INSOMNIACS.

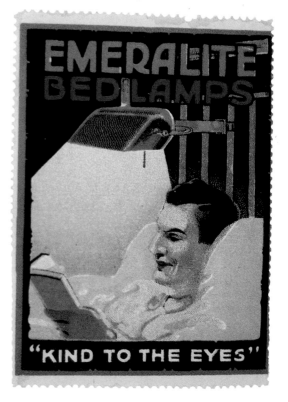

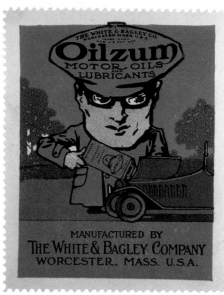

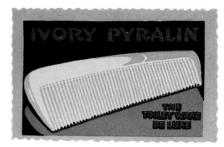

ABOVE: BIG-HEADED WHITE & BAGLEY OILZUM, CLEANZUM, AND SELLZUM.
BELOW: FAITHFUL DISPLAY OF EARLY PLASTIC TOILET ARTICLES FOR THE WELL-GROOMED.

ABOVE: COMIC WAYS TO VIEW LIFE'S
SERIOUS RISKS. RIGHT: HUMANOID LOGOS
OF FRUITS AND CANDIES IN THE CLASSIC
ADVERTISING TRADITION.

FOUR GOOD QUALITIES OF VALENTINE'S PAINTS
SPELLED OUT IN GRAPHIC DETAIL IN THIS SET.

RIGHT TOP: HOWARD CHANDLER CHRISTY'S
DETAILED PEN AND INK DRAWING MAKES TIME FOR
ELGIN. MIDDLE: GENIE'S MAGIC LIGHTS UP THE NIGHT.
BOTTOM: GYPSUM COMPANY'S ANSWER TO THE FIFTY-
FOOT WOMAN—PREPOSTEROUS SCALE TO SELL
CONCRETE BLOCKS.

IRONY, WIT, AND FUN typify a good proportion of the best advertising stamps. Depicted in this chapter are images that signaled a certain characteristic of modern ad psychology—sympathetic advertising through humor and laughter. From the perspective of hindsight these stamps seem incongruous for their time, but advertising was in its infancy and there were no roadmaps to direct one to a successful campaign. Naive artists exposed their innocence to an unsophisticated viewer. That is why poster stamps worked and why they seem so strange seven decades later. The comic approach softened the hard sell. Clichés and visual puns that worked then still work now, transcending language and time. The universality of this rich visual art form speaks to us all. Today ads are test-marketed,

VISUAL CLICHES SOMETIMES MAKE STRONG POSTERS THAT GO THE DISTANCE.

researched, revamped, and redesigned according to viewer and user polls, resulting in images that are homogenized by committee. The humble poster stamp was visualized by artists who were able to translate their style onto paper without much fanfare. The more we know, the more we find that we don't know. The opposite of that appears to have had validity: the less the artists knew, the purer their art form was. No one was certain what motivated people to buy a particular product, what colors affected their choice, or even what "corporate identity" was. This primitive style of early advertising flew by the proverbial seat of its pants, relying on simple humor, unusual juxtaposition, or strange new relationships to create a landscape foreign in visual scope yet universal in appeal.

AN ESOTERIC RARITY AMONG POSTER STAMP COLLECTIBLES–
A 1915–1916 CALENDAR SEWN TO A STAMP SERVING ARMOUR'S STAR HAM.

43

RIGHT:
McMillan's
Pork products,
imitating
illustrator
Coles Phillips's
fadeaway style,
present sizzling
sausages maid to
order. Far right:
That ham
spotlighted
on stage hits
the delicate
balance between
product and
image right on
the nose.

FAR LEFT: Those
ducks won't be
flying high for
long if that
shotgun powder
lives up to its
name. LEFT: If
the hunter can
shoot out small
type at that
distance, those
ducks are
dinner in this
conceptual
design.

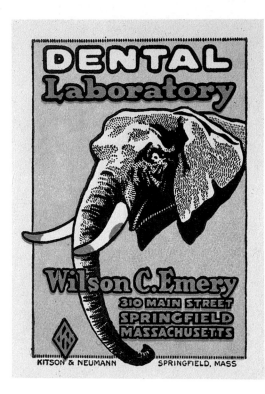

ABOVE: THE MOOD IS SET IN THIS SPARE DESIGN AS UPPER CRUST
MINGLES WITH LOW LIFE. LEFT: NOTHING IS TOO OBVIOUS–
IVORY TUSKS FOR A DENTAL LAB, A GIRAFFE SELLING NECKWEAR.
DEALER TAG BELOW THE GIRAFFE WAS TO BE USED FOR A
DEPARTMENT STORE IMPRINT.

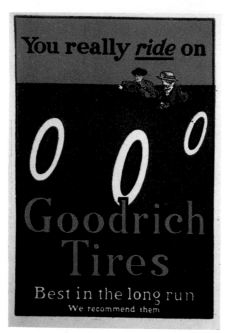

AN UNTIRED VISUAL FOR
A THOUGHT-PROVOKING SLOGAN.

NASTY ACCIDENT INSURES
WORK FOR GERMAN BODY SHOP.

FROTHING DOG CAN TASTE
LEATHER A TREE LIMB AWAY.

FRIGHTENED MOTHER CONFRONTS
TEARFUL CHILD NOT USED TO
LIFE'S SHARP EDGES.

SILHOUETTE POSTER STAMPS,
DESIGNED BY F.S. CHURCH,
ILLUSTRATED COMMON
RAILWAY EXPRESSIONS.

PRINTED BY STROBRIDGE LITHO
OF CIRCUS POSTER FAME, THIS STAMP
IS EVIDENCE OF EARLY REFERENCE
MATERIAL FOR ALFRED E. NEWMAN,
A CHARACTER POPULARIZED BY
MAD MAGAZINE IN THE FIFTIES.

ABOVE LEFT: LARGE PORTIONS
ASSURED BY FERRIS PRODUCTS ARE THE
EXPECTATION OF THIS GRAND GOURMET.
ABOVE RIGHT: SUSPENDED REALITY. FALSE
TEETH ARE ALWAYS A GOOD SIGHT GAG,
EVEN IN THIS SURREAL PORTRAIT. LEFT:
DESPITE A DISAGREEABLE SUMMER, THE
ADVERTISING VALUE OF THIS STAMP
DELIVERED A LARGE INFLUX OF
VISITORS IN 1915.

As the industrial revolution kicked into high gear, the public's awareness of movement was expedited by poster stamps. Motor cars and auto shows, airplanes and exotic destinations, ships and foreign ports, trains and faraway stations all traveled the colorful landscapes of these stamps. A series of stamps with explosive color demonstrated twelve possible uses for Caterpillar tractors, while the future was merely guessed at in German stamps featuring the history of transportation—turning fantasy into reality. With a new age dawning, the diminutive poster stamp opened wide the eyes of a curious public that may never have experienced the various modes of travel these seals displayed. Cars were still a luxury, not yet a necessity. Ship cruises were only for the very wealthy, while flying had just recently crossed the minds of the inventive Wright brothers. These stamps fueled the inspiration of young and old alike. Imaginations soared as collectors accumulated exciting new images from the machine age. Tourist attractions enclosed poster stamps in advertising brochures and guide books sent to potential visitors. Cities eager to reel in tourist dollars illustrated various attractive attributes of their locales. Hotels, travel agencies, and transportation companies distributed stamps directly to those who would benefit from the promotion. Through controlled circulations, advertisers reached their market en masse in a limited way with one big promotional blast or trickled the seals out over a longer period of time. Either way the lure of the unknown fed hungry imaginations ripe with wanderlust. The have-nots could become the haves through the world of poster stamps.

SUGGESTIVE TRAINS AND TUNNELS HAD THE RAILROAD INDUSTRY DREAMING OF BIG BUSINESS.

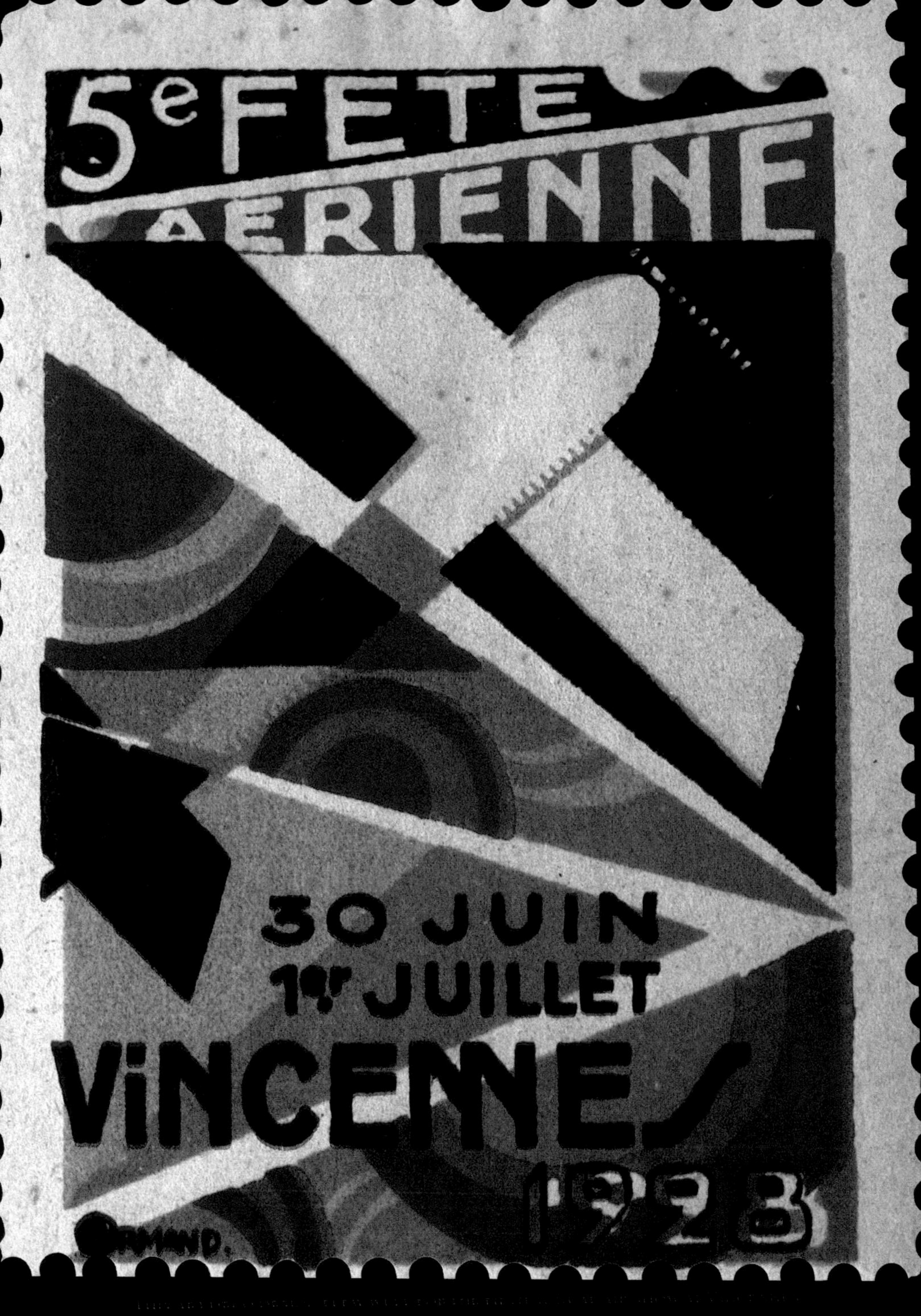
5e FETE AERIENNE
30 JUIN
1er JUILLET
VINCENNES
1928

THE INDUSTRIAL REVOLUTION GAVE US NEW
FREEDOMS OF THE ROAD AS WE MOVED FROM
CARRIAGES TO CARS. ONE OF THE FEW WAYS TO
ADVERTISE NEW CARS IN FULL COLOR WAS ON
POSTER STAMPS—WITH LIST PRICES.

That Good

GULF
GASOLINE

Anti-Knock Quality ~ At No Extra Cost
GULF REFINING COMPANY

BOSCH MAGNETOS WON THE 500 MILE SWEEPSTAKES OF COURSE

BOSCH MAGNETOS WON VANDERBILT CUP RACE 1915 GRAND PRIZE CUP RACE BE SATISFIED · SPECIFY BOSCH IGNITION

CHICAGO'S FIRST INTERNATIONAL 500 MILE AUTO·RACE JUNE 19 1915 SPEEDWAY PARK CHICAGO
GENERAL OFFICES, MARQUETTE BUILDING, CHICAGO

TOP: THERE WAS NO KNOCKING GULF'S AMIABLE STATION ATTENDANT AND HIS SATISFIED CUSTOMER, WHO ADVERTISED THE RELIABILITY AND AFFORDABILITY OF GAS. LEFT AND ABOVE: SPONSORSHIP OF AUTO RACES DATES BACK THIS FAR, AND WINNING THE RACE ENSURES PRODUCT VISIBILITY. THE NOVELTY IN 1915 WOULD LATER BECOME THE SPORT.

TRAVEL AGENTS AND SHIPPING LINES PROMOTED TOURISM
AND FOREIGN TRAVEL VIA POSTER STAMPS.

SERENE SETTINGS ENTICED LANDLUBBERS TO VENTURE SEAWARD
TO DISCOVER NEW SIGHTS IN THE GRAND STYLE.

WAIT!
YOU MAY LOSE

CROSS CROSSINGS CAUTIOUSLY

ARA© 1924

The Sales Printing Corporation New York

TRAIN TRAVEL OFFERED A LEISURELY LOOK AT THE SCENIC BEAUTY OF THE COUNTRY WHILE PROVIDING THE COMFORTS OF HOT MEALS AND A PLACE TO SLEEP. POSTER STAMPS HEAVILY PROMOTED THE USE OF THIS FORM OF TRANSPORTATION WELL INTO THE FORTIES.

AVIATION TOPICALS ARE A MUCH-SOUGHT-AFTER GROUP OF POSTER STAMPS.
THE PAN AMERICAN STAMP IS THOUGHT TO BE THE FIRST LUGGAGE STICKER EVER MADE.
ZEPPELINS ARE AN EVEN MORE SPECIFIC CATEGORY WITH HEAVY INTEREST.

THIS SCARCE SET OF COMMEMORATIVE POSTER STAMPS DETAILS ITALO BALBO'S
GOODWILL ROME-TO-CHICAGO FLIGHT. THE DESIGN AND USE OF METALLIC INKS
MAKE THESE DECO-STYLED AVIATION SEALS MORE APPEALING.

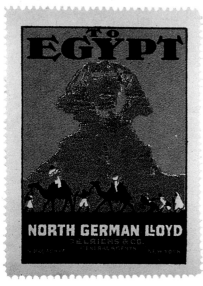

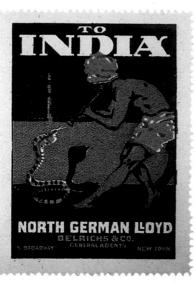

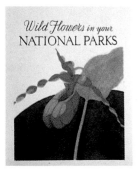

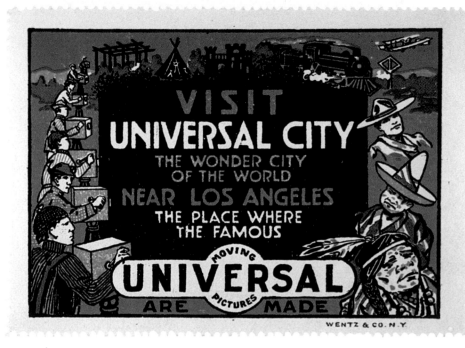

CITIES, PARKS, STATES, AND COUNTRIES TRIED TO CULTIVATE TOURIST DOLLARS WITH COLORFUL DEPICTIONS AND SUPERLATIVE SLOGANS. THE SLOGAN OF EUGENE, OREGON, MEANT SOMETHING FAR DIFFERENT FROM TODAY'S NUCLEAR CONNOTATION.

ONE OF THE EARLIEST USES for poster stamp advertising was the dissemination of information about upcoming exhibitions in the various halls and auditoriums of the day. The dates of these events were on most of the stamps, creating valuable and historic timepieces for present-day collectors. Poster stamps were intended as added publicity for such annual events as industrial fairs, motor shows, or handicraft exhibitions, for they announced such events well before the opening day. These small advertisements became constant reminders throughout the year as collectors tended to peruse their stamp books regularly. This type of stamp also lent itself well to a broader application. An industry could tell its history in a full series of commemoratives. The development of a product or a modern invention

THE OFFICIAL STAMP OF THE 1912 OLYMPICS
IN STOCKHOLM, SWEDEN,
DESIGNED BY OLLE HJORTZBERG,
WAS REJECTED BY SOME
COUNTRIES BECAUSE OF ITS NUDITY.

suggested subjects that could be dramatized to build a background of public interest in an exhibition. By issuing an interesting commemorative series wide advance publicity was arranged, and that alone encouraged attendance. Poster stamps in book or series form were sold at the exhibition or fair as inexpensive souvenirs, to later reinvigorate the memory of a time well spent. A stamp printed in 1845 to celebrate a Viennese exposition may very well have been the beginning of this particular hobby. By no means the pursuit of an isolated group of studious iconoclasts, it was the public at large who was infected with this collecting fever. All of popular culture eagerly embraced the poster stamp as it ushered in the modern age of advertising. The captive audience was in its grasp and now became fascinated.

EXPOSICION
INTERNACIONAL
BARCELONA 1929

THOMAS · S. A. BARCELONA

THE STATUESQUE FEMALE FIGURE GREETING VISITORS TO BARCELONA, SPAIN, AROUSED SOME CONCERN,
BUT THE GARISH COLOR POSTERIZATION DIFFUSED ANY PERCEPTION OF REALITY.

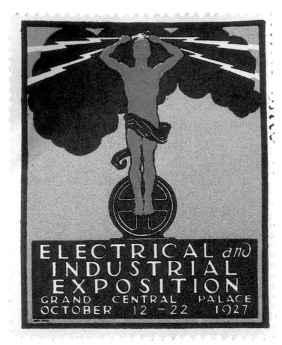

MAJOR INTERNATIONAL DESTINATIONS PUBLICIZED THE EXISTENCE
OF FAIRS AND CARNIVALS USING POSTER STAMPS AS THEIR VEHICLE.

EVERY STYLE OF DESIGN AND ILLUSTRATION WAS USED TO DRAW ATTENTION, FROM THE
SPARSELY DECORATED TO A RECTANGLE PACKED FULL WITH IMAGERY AND RIOTOUS COLOR.

SP🌟RTS ACTIVITIES

ANOTHER OF LIFE'S PLEASURES that poster stamps helped to popularize was the field of sports and associated physical activities. Some of the more valuable seals remain the ones detailing the Olympic games, the pinnacle of international sporting events and global unity. The worldly poster stamp found itself the easiest souvenir to collect, trade, and mail via envelope or postcard to friends and family back home. Whether the stamps showed someone skiing an untouched mountain trail or kicking a brand new pigskin, they were used to make sports equipment and events known to an ignorant public. Image and prestige have always been an important subtext to the concept of advertising. By the novel use of color and context, poster stamps imbued a sense of status to the products and companies they illustrated. That kind of power was back in the hands of the commercial artist. The persuasive image was more of a by-product of poster stamps than a direct intention. Illustrators and draftsmen simply did what they were best at doing. There was no market research at the time to prove why one color attracted attention or why a particular design was effective. But one thing was certain: these unsung artists could really draw and paint. Very quickly they came to understand the primitive printing process, the art of the poster stamp, and the power of persuasion. National sports and sporting events took heed, favoring dispersion of information via advertising seals.

CRT D'ÉTAT DE L'ÉDUCATION PHYSIQUE

3e SALON INTERNATIONAL DES SPORTS
TOURISME ET INDUSTRIES ANNEXES
GRAND PALAIS - CHAMPS ÉLYSÉES
29 OCTOBRE AU 11 NOVEMBRE 1931
Commissariat Général : 21. Av. Champs Élysées - Paris

SCHWEIZ

WINTERSPORT IN GRAUBÜNDEN

LEARN TO BOWL
LEARN TO BOWL WEEK
FREE INSTRUCTION BY EXPERTS
SPONSORED BY THE BOWLING PROPRIETORS ASSOCIATION OF AMERICA

MAY 21-28
NATIONAL TENNIS WEEK

A Case of Good Judgment
Edelweiss BEER

BAZAR NÜRNBERG
Winter-Sport Ausrüstung
BERLIN, Französischestr. 17

SANDERS ENGRAVING CO.
ST. LOUIS

wake up! play
TEN-PINN-ET

"Chums"
BRUNSWICK-BALKE-COLLENDER CO

$500 PRIZE
LABOR DAY OPEN TO ALL
NATIONAL ROWBOAT DERBY
WINNEBAGOLAND
Address Secretary at Oshkosh, Wisconsin

BEAUTY MAY ONLY BE SKIN DEEP, but people were as fashion-conscious at the beginning of the century as we are today. Haberdashers outfitted stylish gentlemen while milliners and seamstresses designed custom creations for the women in vogue. Beauty was no longer just in the eye of the beholder but in the latest jar of cream guaranteed to make wrinkles and liver spots vanish. Poster stamps exposed popular culture to the merits of a new wardrobe, the warmth of a mink coat, the cavalier air of a cravat tucked neatly under a satin smoking jacket. There was no better way to advertise in color while magazines were still monochromatic. Department stores spent lots of money imprinting their own names and addresses on generic fashion stamps to impress potential customers. To capture someone's attention, it seemed better to whisper, and poster stamps were like a whisper to the scream of 24-sheet billboards so plentiful in that era. Dressed fit to kill or dressed for bedtime, these stamps were the fashion catalogs, showing elegant formal wear for a swinging night on the town as well as illustrating comfortable pajamas for that stylish one-third of our lives. Other than to see the items in person at local stores and boutiques, poster stamps were one of the few ways for shoppers to visualize them in color. Early apparel advertising was generally printed in black and white, hardly the ultimate way to spark the style consciousness of potential customers. The whimsical poster stamp may have started a trend toward consumerism, a trend that we still give in to today, lending credence to the theory that advertising has always been a successful medium in attracting the public.

LITHESOME LADIES RIDE AS PART OF
A PARADE IN A FESTIVAL OF FLOWERS
IN GENEVA, 1926.

GOOD CLOTHES for MEN

Capper & Capper

DAPPER WRAPPER FROM CAPPER & CAPPER OUTFITS
THE STYLISH MAN OF THE ROARING TWENTIES.

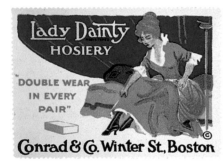

A THING OF BEAUTY IS A JOY TO BEHOLD,
AND SO ARE THESE STAMPS, ADVERTISING
THE SAME THINGS THEN THAT MAKE
WOMEN BEAUTIFUL TODAY.

Suit-ability We have it

Macartney's Apparel Shop

Smart Hats for wise heads

McNeil, McLean & Garland

KETTERLINUS LITHOGRAPHIC MFG CO PHILADELPHIA PENNA

O'Sullivan's HEELS OF NEW LIVE RUBBER

SEVEN LEAGUE BOOTS WHEN O'Sullivanized

THE WELL-DRESSED MAN WAS VISUALLY ASSAULTED
FROM HEAD TO HEEL IN ELEGANT POSTER STAMPS
THAT DISPLAY POPULAR SARTORIAL FASHIONS
AND ATTITUDES.

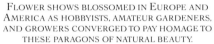

FLOWER SHOWS BLOSSOMED IN EUROPE AND
AMERICA AS HOBBYISTS, AMATEUR GARDENERS,
AND GROWERS CONVERGED TO PAY HOMAGE TO
THESE PARAGONS OF NATURAL BEAUTY.

LOOKING FOR THE PROPER COMBINATION OF
CLOTHES, SCENTS, AND HOME REMEDIES,
CONSUMERS WERE FACED WITH THE PROBLEM
OF MAKING THE OLD LOOK NEW AGAIN.

ACTORS ARE SAID not to like being upstaged by children and animals, but it is just these attention-grabbers that the advertising industry has perennially used to pull on the heartstrings of a susceptible public. The innocence and playfulness of a child and the unconditional love that comes from a pet serve as powerful emotional triggers to persuade a customer to buy a product. Poster stamp artists preyed upon this response mechanism to sell everything from tires to oatmeal and from appliances to visiting the zoo. These designs were freer and the tone not so serious as in other topical stamps. Poster stamps lent themselves well to the use of this subject matter, for the simplicity of design and bold application of color were reminiscent of children's book illustrations of that time—stylized, graphic, and quickly understood. Also, children collected these stamps as well, so that both the image and the message had to reach a youthful market, the possible future buyers of goods and services. But poster stamp advertising was not wasted on the youth. Animals and children symbolized strength, goodness, foresight, and other virtures that were not easily described in the usual visual translations. Animals were given desirable human qualities and attributes, much as those early Walt Disney animators gave personalities to their well-loved cartoon characters. Children were portrayed with wide grins as they clearly enjoyed the product the stamp was advertising. Parents, eager to please their own family members, were suckered into purchasing anything to "keep up with the Joneses."

THE GENTLEMAN OF THE BARNYARD,
DRESSED IN COLORFUL OVERALLS
CAUGHT READERS' ATTENTION—A
CASE OF TRUE ANIMAL HUSBANDRY.

WHAT CHILD HASN'T DIPPED A FINGER INTO A SWEET JAR OF PRESERVES? IN CLASSIC
ILLUSTRATIVE STYLE, A STRONG EMOTIONAL RESPONSE IS APTLY CAPTURED FOR BEECH-NUT.

The animal kingdom
provided a wealth of spokesmen to sell
everything from shoes to chewing gum. Sometimes the
creatures were given human characteristics.

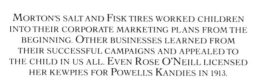

MORTON'S SALT AND FISK TIRES WORKED CHILDREN
INTO THEIR CORPORATE MARKETING PLANS FROM THE
BEGINNING. OTHER BUSINESSES LEARNED FROM
THEIR SUCCESSFUL CAMPAIGNS AND APPEALED TO
THE CHILD IN US ALL. EVEN ROSE O'NEILL LICENSED
HER KEWPIES FOR POWELL'S KANDIES IN 1913.

PROTECTING THE FAMILY AND EDUCATING THE CHILDREN ARE PRIORITIES FOR PARENTS. THE STAMPS SHOWN HERE INSURE A SAFE AND SECURE FUTURE IF YOU SUPPORT THE BUSINESS ADVERTISED.

A GOOD SALESMAN WILL SELL ANYTHING if it's given the right promotion. Smart companies virtually guaranteed the success of a national promotion or a local show by issuing poster stamps to whet the public's omnivorous appetite for what's new or what's next. Poster stamp topics were seemingly unlimited. One very popular category in the late 1930s and early '40s was the celebration of "the week." There was Cat Week, Dog Week, National Farm Safety Week, and so on. Fried dough even got a boost as National Donut Week promotion was set in motion via poster stamps. Few people would have known about the Dairy Show except for the graphic stamps that showed a tethered cow's head as part of a beautiful design. Perennial flower shows sprouted

A MODERN MADONNA AND CHILD
SOLICIT CONTRIBUTIONS FOR HEALTH
IN THE 1922 CHRISTMAS SEAL DRIVE.

colorful bouquets on the still-life canvases of poster stamps, making them another highly collectible topic of the hobby. Many charities have sold poster stamps to raise funds or to solicit contributions in connection with holidays. The best-known campaigns are the Easter and Christmas seals, which are international in scope and collected by philatelists. The use of these stamps on correspondence extends the appeal of the campaign and gets the message of the charity drive into wide circulation. But colorful holiday stamps have been used to decorate otherwise-plain envelopes and spread the festive holiday spirit. Predating transparent tape, holiday seals were also used as a practical and decorative means of holding together tissue-wrapped gift packages.

THE MODERN
ALADDIN

AMERICA'S
ELECTRICAL
W E E K
DEC. 2 to 9
1 9 1 6

DO IT ELECTRICALLY!

THE REVOLUTIONARY MAGIC OF ELECTRICITY IS PROMOTED JUST IN TIME FOR THE
HOLIDAY CELEBRATIONS, USING ALADDIN AND HIS GENIE AS APPROPRIATE SYMBOLS.

THE HOLIDAY SEASON LOOSENED CONSUMER PURSE STRINGS, WITH STAMPS COAXING PEOPLE TO REMEMBER FAVORITE CHARITIES AS WELL AS THE FAMILY—THE DUAL FINANCIAL TUG OF DECEMBER PROMOTIONS. NOTE ROCKWELL KENT'S FAMOUS CHRISTMAS SEAL ANGEL OF 1939.

AN EARLY SUNKIST PROMOTION INCLUDED BOTH
ORANGE AND LEMON CITRUS CROPS, WITH A LOVELY
YOUNG GIRL SHOWING OFF THE FRUITS OF HER
LABOR. THE CIRCULAR STAMP WAS A NOVEL SHAPE
PERFECTLY SUITED TO THE PRODUCT.

STAMPS ALERTED CONSUMERS TO EVERYTHING FROM MILK TO MAN'S BEST FRIEND, FROM FATHER'S DAY TO DOOMSDAY, REMINDING US TO EAT SOMETHING IN BETWEEN.

MANY COMPANIES issued series of stamps that broadcast all facets of their products to a curious public. They were produced one at a time and distributed at regular intervals, prompting the collector to look forward with anticipation to the newest release. Poster stamps were also printed as an entire sheet of diverse images and sold at once. Either way the composite strengthened the appeal in color and design. The common thread through them all might have been only a company's logo, a similar color combination, or a design format. The fever to collect every last one of a series has kept the interest going over the years among hobbyists. The fact that undamaged sheets of perforated stamps still are found is a tribute to the careful way people saved their poster stamps in those days. Fragile even then, they were kept in glassine sleeves in specially made books, and they are even more fragile now. In current trading circles, relatively few sheets have the dog-earred corners one might expect of paper goods fifty to eighty years old. Single stamps turn up now and again, even the rare ones, but full sheets in good condition have become highly collectible. Few of the collectors of full sheets in the stamps' heyday could have foreseen increased popularity and value more than half a century later. Andy Warhol made us aware of the powerful effect of serial imagery through his silk-screened artwork. Pop culture meets pop art once again in the repetitive imagery on poster stamps.

THE QUAKER OATS STORYBOOK SERIES APPEALED TO BOTH CHILD AND ADULT COLLECTORS.

MOST POPULAR BICYCLE WRENCH IN THE WORLD

"STERLING"

MOSSBERG GUARANTEED WRENCHES & TOOLS

FRANK MOSSBERG CO · ATTLEBORO · MASS

MOSSBERG MASTER TOOLS "FORD NECESSITIES"

FRANK MOSSBERG CO. ATTLEBORO. MASS.

FOR MOTORISTS & ENGINEERS ON LAND OR SEA

MOSSBERG SOCKET WRENCH SET NO. 14

FRANK MOSSBERG CO. ATTLEBORO

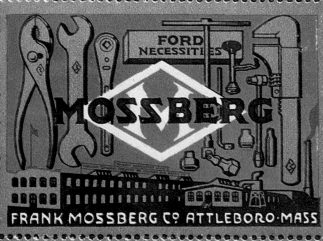

FORD NECESSITIES

MOSSBERG

FRANK MOSSBERG C° ATTLEBORO · MASS

THE CLEVEREST TOOLS FOR MOTORCYCLES

SOCKET WRENCH SET NO. 5

ENGINEERS' WRENCH SET NO. 715

76

MOSSBERG GUARANTEED WRENCHES & TOOLS ATTLEBORO - MASS

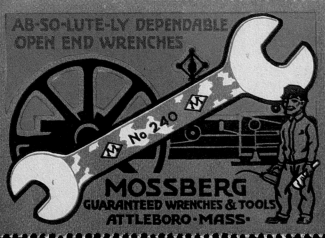

AB-SO-LUTE-LY DEPENDABLE OPEN END WRENCHES

No 240

MOSSBERG GUARANTEED WRENCHES & TOOLS ATTLEBORO · MASS ·

INCREDIBLE DIVERSITY AND DETAIL WERE OBTAINED USING BASIC PRINTING FUNDAMENTALS, BUT BY THE INVENTIVE USE OF THREE COLORS, MOSSBERG TOOLS SOLD QUALITY AND FED INFORMATION TO THE POTENTIAL BUYER.

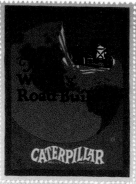

THE RANGE OF STYLES AND THE VARIATIONS OF THEMES CREATE
VISUAL WALLS OF COLOR TO SELL MYRIAD PRODUCTS.

NOT ONLY EMERALITE LAMPS BUT EAGLE MILK'S POSTERIZED SERIES AND
BOSTON NOZZLE'S REPEATED IMAGES WERE ALL "KIND TO THE EYES."

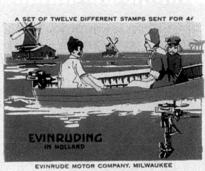

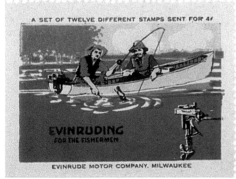

EVINRUDING AROUND THE WORLD—THE LITTLE ENGINE THAT COULD.

THE POSTER STAMPS OF WORLD WAR II represented the last great hurrah for this form of printed ephemera. Full-size propaganda posters were plentiful during this fearful time; loose lips sank ships and the walls had ears, but everyone's eyes were on the patriotic poster stamp that was capable of conveying a message of hope and hate directly to every mailbox in America. There was nothing to conflict or compete with that message, for these advertising seals had the added merit of being independent of other advertising. They did not rely on good placement in a given publication or on outdoing the competition in any periodical. When they arrived glued to an envelope or invoice, they got full attention. Poster stamps helped national and civic organizations in their appeal to the public in such matters as safety first, saving and recycling products during wartime, recruiting, and even peace. The peace stamps, although not very common, spread the idea that "war would cease if you favored world peace." In contrast, the government's War Production Board issued miniature versions of numerous propaganda posters. While this poor man's art gallery is part of our rich cultural heritage, it is also a reminder that we can be our own worst enemy—the only way to win this game is not to play. If anyone doubted that advertising could persuade people to action, the power of propaganda stamps was the proof of it. The images were very small, but they were loaded with all the emotion that war brings out in people. These stamps did not ride the sensitive line but used extremes to urge action.

AMERICA HONORS CHINA IN THE CAUSE OF FREEDOM IN THIS POWERFUL GRAPHIC DESIGNED BY LUDWIG STAEHLE.

STILL
MORE
PRODUCTION

ACTION WAS CALLED FOR AND A STAND
WAS TO BE TAKEN. THERE WAS NO MIDDLE
GROUND WITH THE WORLD AT WAR.

WITH A COUNTRY COMMITTED TO THE TASK AT HAND,
VICTORY WAS ASSURED. SADLY, IT TOOK A WORLD WAR
TO CREATE A UNITED NATION.

ACKN^OWLEDGMENTS

S PECIAL THANKS to Allene Rose for sharing her collection and for taking me to that first stamp show; to Ewald Van Elkan for sharing his knowledge, interest, time, and stamps; to Leonard Stark for his valuable information and desire to help; to Walton Rawls, Deborah Sloan, and Hope Koturo for their care and belief in me and my product; Drew Andresen and Andresen Typographics for keeping aesthetics and craftsmanship in typography alive; Jeff Spielberg; Roger and Bonnie Riga; Ty Wood; Nick Follansbee; Walter Schmidt; George Theofiles; Christensen and Stone; William & Daily Books; Steve Turner; Suzie Brownstein; Kate Hendrickson; Westland Graphics; Jeffrey Fey; Jim Heimann; Doug Taylor; Sarah Jane Freymann; and finally, to Fiona for allowing me the time to pursue my passions.

For further information on poster stamp collecting, dealers, and clubs:

Poster Stamp Society of America
3654 Applegate Road
Jacksonville, Oregon 97530

Cinderella Publications
3654 Applegate Road
Jacksonville, Oregon 97530

Ewald Van Elkan
4 Christopher Way
Anniston, Alabama 36201

Cinderella Co.
P.O. Box 265
Sykesville, Maryland 21784

Rigastamps
P.O. Box 326
Eaton, Ohio 45320

Robert DuBoise
838 Temple Road
Pottstown, Pennsylvania 19464

Leonard Stark
247 E. Chestnut
Chicago, Illinois 60611

1871 Shop
Attn: Don Reuter   Drawer #E
South Lyon, Michigan 48178